Three-Dimensional Followership:

Finding Success When Others Are Driving

First Printing: 2018

ISBN 978-0-578-60281-3

Chapter 1: This is a Book About What?

During a denominational church meeting a few years ago, I made a statement about being excited to be "a Pip." At the time there were four African Methodist Episcopal (AME) Church pastors in the in Shreveport and it so happened that one was female and the rest of us were male. Because of this ratio, the fact that all our names started with the letter "P," and that the female pastor led the largest denominational church in the area, we took to calling ourselves "Gladys Knight and the Pips." When I told our area leadership that "I was proud to be a Pip", I was stating the fact that it was great to be part of the AME team in Shreveport and that I looked forward to carrying on in that role. While I was patting myself on the back for celebrating teamwork within the church, I noticed that my comment wasn't as well received as I expected. "Why would you want to be a Pip?", I was asked. I was told that I should want to be a leader and not just a follower. Admittedly, I was surprised by this reaction, but those words were very similar to those spoken in my past as others celebrated the role of the leader while openly denigrating the idea of being a follower. Since that occurrence, I've become hypersensitive to what people say about both leadership and followership. I enthusiastically wrote my first book, *Three-Dimensional Leadership*, to provide my view of what it takes to be a successful leader. Again, I patted myself on the back for putting something out to the masses that everyone could read, learn and apply. However, something was still missing.

In April 2018, about six months after *Three-Dimensional Leadership* came out, I discovered that missing piece. During one of the plenary sessions at the "15th Annual Males of Color Empowerment Seminar" in Detroit, the speaker talked boldly about leadership and relationships which was right up my alley. Then she made a statement that rocked my world. She asked the simple question, "Who has ever taught you about followership?" In the vein of the jet.com TV commercials, my mind was blown off and purple powder was spewing all over the room. What shocked me more than her question was that she never referred to followership again. Her statement forced me to look back critically at all the leadership training I received throughout my life to see what I had learned about followership. Starting with Air Force Junior ROTC at Niceville High School, to Air Force ROTC at the University of South Alabama to 24 years as an Air Force officer including 3 years teaching leadership at Air Force ROTC Detachment 605, North Carolina A&T State University; I had spent the majority of my life learning about, practicing and teaching others about leadership. During those years I probably heard someone say a thousand times, "If you're going to be a good leader, you must be a good follower". Then, in each of those thousand times the speaker went on to talk about being a leader and never broached the follower subject again. As a person who doesn't believe in coincidence, I have to think these oversights were intentional, but the question is, "Why?" Could it be that being a follower is so easy that we don't feel anyone needs to learn how to do it? That can't be the answer because we make the point that every leader must be a "good" follower and not simply "a follower." Therefore, if we are going to apply a modifier like "good" to something, shouldn't we provide direction to accomplish that goal? Perhaps we gloss over followership because there is such a negative stigma to being a follower that nobody wants to take the time to discuss the subject. After all, as several people have implied to me over the years, "Why would someone want to be a follower at all, much less a good one?" I did a search at www.brainyquote.com to find a few thoughts about being a follower, and outside of those talking about their preferences and religious beliefs, here's what I found[1]:

- I'm a shepherd, not a sheep, and I've always prided myself on being a leader and not a follower. – Actor Dustin Diamond
- I consider myself a leader. I am not a follower.— Professional football player Stefon Diggs
- I'm not a follower. I'm a leader. And anyone who speaks their mind is always criticized. – Musician Tyler, the Creator

---

[1] https://www.brainyquote.com/topics/follower, accessed August 3, 2018.

- I was born a leader, never a follower. I never felt peer pressure. If the group goes left, I go right. – Boxer Deontay Wilder
- My dad taught me to be a leader or a follower, and he said follower ain't fun. So I want to be the leader of Bubba Watson. – Golfer Bubba Watson
- The purpose of a politician is to be a leader. A politician has to lead. Otherwise he's just a follower. – Economist Alan Greenspan
- All these boundaries - Africa, Asia, Malaysia, America - are set by men. But you don't have to look at boundaries when you are looking at a man - at the character of a man. The question is: What do you stand for? Are you a follower, or are you a leader? – Basketball player Hakeem Olajuwon

While I could probably search other places and find seven other quotes that speak to the virtues of being a follower…then again, I'm not so sure about that…I would argue that the vast majority of society would nod their heads emphatically to those seven statements. We want leaders. We want to be leaders. To be a follower is to accept being "the tail and not the head" as some of my more religious friends would say.

It is because of these questions and this negative perception of followers that I have decided to write this book. I made the case in *Three-Dimensional Leadership* that every area of society is calling out for better leaders. However, as I talk to employers and reflect back on my time in the Air Force and in the church, I believe there is another call going out from the front offices, boardrooms and HR departments. That call is, "Bring me better followers." In addition to needing people to cast a vision and change the direction of their companies, everyone, from the largest mega corporation to the smallest mom and pop grocery store, is looking for people who can do the legwork to make the leader's vision a reality and put those changes into effect. Regular, run-of-the-mill followers, won't do. The world needs good followers, those men and women who sit in the proverbial backseat of the car while others drive but who make a world of difference to the quality of the trip.

Before I dive into this uncommon concept, I want to explain why this is three-dimensional followership. As leaders must interact with the task, the team and themselves to be successful; so must followers navigate these same three areas to be their best. Shortcomings in any of these areas puts the follower in danger of a pink slip and the team or organization in danger of failure. We've all worked with that guy who doesn't get any work done. No matter how low we set the bar, he continually manages to come in under it. There's no way you can call yourself a good follower if you can't complete a task. Therefore, a three-dimensional follower must understand the GOAL of the task. However, if the follower can complete a task but has an attitude that drags the team down, that's not a good follower either. Think about the coworker who is all about business and isn't there to make friends. Sure, she gets the job done but nobody in the organization wants anything to do with her; which destroys any synergy the team could get from having multiple people available to conquer a task. Those of us who want to be better followers, needs to know her ROLE on the team. Finally, a follower must know their SOUL. As with the requirement for leaders to PREPARE to make themselves to be a success, followers must understand themselves to be effective members of successful organizations.

As I type this I can hear the hairs on many necks bristling at the idea that they are reading a book encouraging people to be better followers. After all, parents are trying to get their kids to be leaders at school and among their friends. A book like this could set the kids back to being tossed and driven by the whims of everyone else. Hopefully, over the huffs and grunts of those disappointed in this topic you can hear me chuckle. Why am I laughing? Because every parent dying for their child to be a leader among their peers is crying out for that same child to be a better follower at home… "Why won't they do their chores?" …"Why don't they clean up after themselves?"…"Why won't they listen to me?" Then again, maybe I'm the only parent or pastor or leader that wants those leaders I am nurturing for greater things in the world to be more diligent followers when I'm in charge. This dichotomy is why I think this subject is so important. While every follower may not become a leader, those followers who get the title, the office, the position and claim the moniker as leader, are still followers. I am the pastor, the leader, of St Mary AME Church in Shreveport. Nevertheless, it is made very clear to me every October at our Annual Conference that I am a follower because in that venue, the Bishop is the leader. The math teacher is the leader of his class but is the follower in relation to the principal. The principal is the leader of the school, but she is the follower of the superintendent of schools. I could go on, but you get the point. EVERY leader is a follower and if the leader forgets that, then the success of the organization is in jeopardy. Therefore, since every person is, and will be, a follower, we all need to learn how to be successful in that role so our teams and organizations can operate at peak efficiency. We have to be contributing members on the drive whether we are behind the steering wheel or sitting in the backseat. And if we aren't careful, by the end of this book, we just might see that there is something to be said for being "a Pip."

Taking a 3-D Look at Yourself

1. Are you a leader or follower?

2. Do you see being a follower as a negative thing?

3. If you see being a follower as a negative thing, how does that view impact your ability to follow others? How do you think that view impacts the ability of others to follow you?

4. What does it mean to be a "good follower?"

Chapter 2: Followers Must Know the GOAL of the Task

People with goals succeed because they know where they are going.
-- Earl Nightingale

Because I am a hyper-competitive person, I have one question whenever someone is teaching me a game for the first time… "How do I win?" Before you tell me the rules, the number of players, the names of the pieces or show me the playing surface, I have to know the GOAL so I can decide if I even want to play the game. This truth played out when I was in graduate school. During that time, I was introduced to the game of Hearts. I had grown up playing Spades and, as you may know, the rules of Spades and Hearts are very similar. Both games involve four players and a standard deck of cards. In each round of the game you are tasked to match the suit that is played. Even though the games seem very similar, the GOAL of the two games is drastically different. In Spades, the GOAL is to collect as many sets of cards (books) as possible so as a player, you want to win each round. However, in Hearts, the GOAL is to collect as few books as possible. (Yes, I know in each game there are special circumstances for not taking any books in Spades or taking all the books in Hearts but those are exceptions to the general rules.) My point is that while playing Hearts, every hand or so I'd forget the GOAL and be very proud of myself for winning a book that I could have easily lost. Because I forgot the GOAL, I wasn't as effective as I could have been.

Hence the situation with many followers. A lot of people are part of teams, organizations and groups but have no idea what the GOAL- "The result or achievement toward which effort is directed"[2] for the task at hand. In actuality, I think this may be a combination of poor followership and lazy leadership. The followers just want to do the bare minimum to punch the clock while the leaders don't think the followers have a need to know the "big picture." Both of these attitudes are detrimental to organizational success. Even though the followers are wearing the right uniform and performing jobs essential to the completion of the organization's greater purpose, their lack of knowledge of the GOAL limits their ability to improve on their part of the process and ultimately improve the team's result. When it comes to a task, good followers must know the GOAL; which for our purposes means knowing the GUIDANCE, the OUTCOME, the ASSIGNMENT and the LINKAGE. The more a follower is familiar with these aspects of a given task, the more likely the follower will succeed and increase the team's opportunities for success.

> *If the staff lacks policy guidance against which to test*
> *decisions, their decisions will be random.*
> *-- Donald Rumsfeld*

---

[2] https://www.dictionary.com/browse/goal, accessed 11 September 2018.

I will not confirm or deny that I know a guy who lives in my house who hates reading directions. He's been known to bring home a bookshelf, a computer or some other item where assembly is required and tear into the boxes and start connecting things without regard to all the paper the manufacturer put in the box. "After all," I might have heard him say, "How hard can this be?" For those of you unlearned in such feats of misplaced self-confidence, the end result is usually a lot of yelling and backtracking on the work previously accomplished. And even if the work is completed and the shelf is standing upright, there's always the question of "Why did they put all these extra pieces in the box?" Without those "extra" pieces, the shelf starts to lean. This is a great picture of where many followers find themselves. They have ignored the GUIDANCE provided by leadership and have set out to complete the task because "they know what they are doing." The follower ends up with a project that looks to be finished but is leaning to one side or the other giving evidence to the fact that the follower didn't take all the necessary steps required by the GUIDANCE.

While GUIDANCE comes in many forms, from the simple directions on the outside of a shampoo bottle to the verbal directives of a coach to the volumes of text contained in tax law, we invariably resist it which is why many of us are not good followers. The bottom line is "we know better" so why should we be confined to the ceaseless chatter of someone else? We have degrees and experience and ideas so we can certainly complete any task without help. That sounds so good because we say it so often but it couldn't be more wrong. In our pride, we act like we are the first individuals to ever take up this task and there's nothing anyone else could tell us that would make this job easier or more productive.

What we miss out on is that GUIDANCE is often the result of multiple failed attempts and years of prior experience. For example, have you ever read a petroleum jelly bottle? If you do, you will see the words, "Don't eat the petroleum jelly." Now when I first noticed the warning I was shocked. Why would the makers of this product actually waste their time spelling out something so simple? Then it hit me…the bottles didn't start with a warning against human ingestion. The warning was in response to people looking for something to go on their toast. Yes, it sounds crazy to many of us but if it wasn't a thing, there wouldn't be a warning against it. The manufacturer provided the GUIDANCE to assure the safe and effective use of the product. Similarly, leaders and organizations provide GUIDANCE along with task assignments to their followers to make available the framework within which the follower can be successful. Failure to follow the GUIDANCE will spell ruin for the follower and eventually for the team. Because many leaders tend to be "idea people," they may not be as familiar with the details and they need followers who are intimately familiar with the rules and GUIDANCE that apply to a particular task. By knowing the GUIDANCE and sharing what they know, these followers become essential elements to the team.

When I was in my high school Junior ROTC class, the instructor gave us a quiz of basic math facts. The caveat was that even through there were 100 questions on the test, we only had 60 seconds to complete it. While the teacher reminded us several times to read the directions, I was devising my battle plan to finish more questions than anyone else. When he gave us permission to start, I flipped my paper over and started writing feverishly. The problems were simple enough but I could feel time sprinting away. Then out of the corner of my eye, I noticed several people turn their paper over and put their heads down on the table. I was pissed. There was no way these people could finish this quiz before me. All of a sudden, the instructor called out time was up and I was exclaimed how unfair the quiz was and that the other folks must have cheated because they finished and I didn't. Calmly, the instructor looked and asked if I had read the directions, and I emphatically I told him that I didn't have time for that. I had to finish the task. He told me to take a moment to read the directions. Incredulously, I began reading and with each word my heart sunk. The directions for the test were, "Answer question number 17, turn your paper over and put your head down on the table." The application here is simple. I decided I knew it all and I ignored the GUIDANCE in front of me and ended up doing more work than necessary and frustrating myself in the process. This is my daily reminder that a follower who takes time to be intimately familiar with the GUIDANCE for a particular task, and shares that knowledge with those around him or her, will make themselves vital members of the team and make team success a more likely result…and won't waste time answering questions that nobody cares about.

To conquer frustration one must remain intensely focused on
the outcome.
-- TF Hodge

As you read this right now, there is a wife giving a task to her husband. Perhaps she wants him to clean the kitchen, do the laundry, or dust the bedroom. Whatever the task, she knows what she wants done and she believes she has made that clear to him. Being a diligent brother, the husband, starts and "finishes" the task. When the wife comes to observe what has been done, there is a noticeable expression of displeasure on her face because while she can tell he did something, he certainly didn't do it to her satisfaction. She might even say something like, "You call this clean?" or "That might be clean to someone else, but it's not clean to me." Then again, maybe I'm the only one who has witnessed this scenario played out (I may or may not be the aforementioned husband in this example). While the husband understood what was supposed to be done, he didn't fully understand the OUTCOME desired by leadership. You see, the husband worked on the task to <u>his</u> satisfaction and considered the task complete. However, since the husband didn't assign the task, the husband cannot be the ultimate determiner of the appropriate OUTCOME for the task. The husband, as the follower, has failed because he didn't provide the OUTCOME specified by the leader. If a follower doesn't know what "done" means, then the follower can't possibly complete the task in a satisfactory manner.

The irony of the follower knowing the OUTCOME is that sometimes it is equally bad to over-perform as it is to underperform. A former supervisor of mine said it this way, "Perfection is the enemy of good enough." He said this to me numerous times because by nature, I am a perfectionist. In my mind, if a job is worth doing, it's worth doing to the nth degree with every i dotted and every t crossed and then throw in some extra i's and t's for good measure. However, when the OUTCOME desired by the boss is a couple of lines handwritten on a piece of paper explaining a subject and you turn in a 30-page dissertation on the topic, you have not met the OUTCOME.

How does a follower learn the OUTCOME of a task? In a perfect world, the leader would specify the OUTCOME so there's no question in the mind of the follower. Unfortunately, every leader hasn't read *Three-Dimensional Leadership* (how's that for a shameless plug?) and they may just assume everyone knows what they mean when they assign a task. In the cases where confusion exists, it's up to a three-dimensional follower to seek out the definition of the desired OUTCOME. This definition can come from the leader or from the GUIDANCE. Please note that I only listed two sources for the OUTCOME. Too often, followers rely on sources outside of the leader and the GUIDANCE and end up disappointing the leader and damaging their credibility as followers. Again, only the one assigning the task can identify the appropriate OUTCOME. Tasks are usually assigned by leaders or GUIDANCE and therefore these should be the only two sources followers reference to determine what "being finished" looks like. Understanding the OUTCOME is important because time is a precious commodity and if you don't have time to do a job right the first time, where will you find time to do it over again. Therefore, before starting the task, a successful follower will make sure she fully comprehends the expectations of the leadership and knows what "done" means. Is an email response good enough or is a signed memo required? Do we need to bring the leadership a final solution or do we need to bring options so the leader can make the decision? Questions like these need to be answered so the follower can finish the assignment in the right amount of time and in the right way.

Perhaps there is nothing more frustrating to a parent than taking a family road trip and hearing the incessant wailing from the backseat with those dreadful four words (say them with me)… "Are we there yet?" I mean, we know we are going on a drive of at least 12 hours and we told them it will be a while before we get there but 20 minutes into the trip they are asking if we've arrived. The kids are letting someone else drive but their sole focus in on the OUTCOME. They want to know what it means for the journey to be complete because they are not just out for a drive. They are trying to get somewhere. While I'm not advocating followers to continually ask their leaders "are we there yet," I am challenging all followers to get a clear view of what the OUTCOME is so they will move in the right direction and be ready to celebrate completion at the right time.

If you're not making use of even the most routine assignment to learn something, realize that many of your colleagues and coworkers are.
-- Adena Friedman

There is a story by an anonymous author about four people named Everybody, Somebody, Anybody, and Nobody.

There was an important job to be done and Everybody was sure that Somebody would do it. Anybody could have done it, but Nobody did it. Somebody got angry about that because it was Everybody's job. Everybody thought that Anybody could do it, but Nobody realized that Everybody wouldn't do it. It ended up that Everybody blamed Somebody when Nobody did what Anybody could have done. I've always loved this story because it points directly at everyone in an organization understanding their ASSIGNMENT. If a follower doesn't know his or her individual ASSIGNMENT on a task, the task is in severe danger of failure.

Like the definition of the OUTCOME, the definition of the ASSIGNMENT should come from the leader. One battle that I've always fought with my own leadership style is just throwing out tasks to those working with me, but not making any specific ASSIGNMENTS. Invariably, as the deadline approached, I would look around to see who completed each part of the task only to discover, everyone went their own way assuming someone else was going to handle what "the boss asked for." (Yes, you can see why I like that story because I've lived it out way too many times.) For people who just want to be followers, my leadership failing is perfect because if they aren't told to do anything, they can just hang around and get paid. However, this book is for three-dimensional followers who want to be better in their current position. Therefore, these followers know to be their best, they need to have a good grasp of their ASSIGNMENT in relation to the task. For that reason, if they work for a leader like me who likes to just throw out things and expect folks to pick up the slack, three-dimensional followers will seek out a specific definition of assignments. This might be as simple as volunteering for the ASSIGNMENT or asking the leader to make appointments as necessary. Yes, I've heard it a thousand times that we shouldn't volunteer for anything. Regrettably, when I haven't volunteered for things that I would have liked to do, I've ended up being "volun-told" to do things I didn't want to do. Either way I ended up with an ASSIGNMENT and in hindsight, I realize that it would have been much better to volunteer for what I wanted to do rather than let someone else decide what I had to do.

The value in followers knowing their ASSIGNMENT is that we can ensure the responsibilities for the entire task are covered. This brings to mind the admonition often repeated but seldom obeyed that people need to "stay in their lanes." When given an ASSIGNMENT, good followers keep their focus on their ASSIGNMENT. Unfortunately, like track, the lines between the lanes are so thin that it's easy to drift into the next lane. However, when followers are so preoccupied on what's happening in every other lane, they are incapable of completing their ASSIGNMENT to the best of their ability. When I was much younger (and thinner) I would run track and much to my dismay, I would seldom win the races. My problem was that even though I was faster than the vast majority of the other runners, I would run the race while trying to look and see what everyone else was doing in their lanes. As you might imagine, it's hard to run at full speed when you are looking around. So while I was looking at the folks in the lane to the left and commenting on their poor running styles, someone would pass me on the right and I'd act bewildered at how that person could beat me. My problem wasn't that I physically left my lane. My problem was that I spent too much time looking into everyone else's lane. If I had just focused on what was going on with my ASSIGNMENT, I would have lived up to my potential.

Please don't misunderstand me. This is not to say that followers shouldn't help others on the team out with their ASSIGNMENTS. We are definitely better when we work together. However, we cannot forsake our ASSIGNMENT to make sure someone else gets their ASSIGNMENT done. If you've ever flown you've heard the flight attendant say, "In the case the cabin loses air pressure, oxygen masks will fall from the ceiling. If you are with someone who needs assistance, PUT YOUR MASK ON FIRST, and then help them." This principle works on an airplane in an emergency and it works in offices and on jobsites around the world. Get your ASSIGNMENT done first before helping someone else because that's your job. Your primary job isn't to help your teammates. Your primary job is to finish your ASSIGNMENT. Once that ASSIGNMENT is finished, you should go help those who haven't finished yet. One last example…when I was in high school, my friend Cris and I were both told by our fathers to cut our yards. Being concerned with efficiency, we decided we would work together and cut both yards together, cutting our work in half. We went to my yard first and finished in record time. It was great. Then we went to his yard and began to cut. We were making great progress but then his lawnmower quit working. We were devastated to realize he had run out of gas and we didn't have any more or a way to get more. When Cris' dad came home to see a half-done yard, I can tell you he wasn't satisfied with the answer, "I helped Bobby cut his yard." His dad wasn't satisfied because Cris' ASSIGNMENT wasn't to cut my dad's yard. His ASSIGNMENT was to cut his dad's yard and because he didn't stay in his lane, the task was left incomplete. Fortunately, life has worked out pretty well for Cris since that moment. I'd like to believe we both learned from that mistake and I'm hoping you'll learn too. Know your ASSIGNMENT, do your ASSIGNMENT and stay in your lane…or you could run out of gas.

Sometimes God presents opportunities that look insignificant or rather ordinary. Perhaps you don't see how they fit into the big picture for your life. But if God is asking you to do something, He has a purpose for it.
-- Victoria Osteen

In a story that is reminiscent of "Undercover Boss," famous architect Christopher Wren went to a work site while workers were building St. Paul's cathedral in London which he had designed. He asked one of the workers, "What are you doing?" and the man replied, "I am cutting a piece of stone." He walked a little further and asked another man the same question and the man replied, "I am earning five shillings, two pence a day." Finally, Mr. Wren went to a third man with the same question and the man answered, "I am helping Sir Christopher Wren build a beautiful cathedral." The difference in the third man from the first two is that the third man saw the LINKAGE between his ASSIGNMENT and the OUTCOME.

One of the biggest challenges for many followers is getting energized about the task they are doing. When they consider the task unimportant or inconsequential, they don't put in all the effort they could and ultimately put the entire effort at risk. Understanding and appreciating the LINKAGE between the ASSIGNMENT given to the follower and the grand OUTCOME of the endeavor is crucial to the efficient completion of the sub-task and the accomplishment of the overall task. This means the follower, as well as the leader, need to have a recognition of the big picture being asked of the team. I know this notion runs counter to the feelings of many in leadership circles because we want those on the lower levels of the corporate ladder to just focus on their jobs and not worry about anything else. Unfortunately, when followers are confined to just viewing their individual jobs, they can develop of sort of tunnel vision that results in a sense of apathy because they don't see the LINKAGE between what they are doing and the forward motion of the organization. Of course, everyone in the organization doesn't need to know every minute detail of what everyone else is doing. After all, the pipefitter doesn't need to know exactly how the financial manager does her job. However, the pipefitter needs to have a solid sense of how what he is doing ultimately impacts the completion the mission. The third man in the Christopher Wren story probably had a minimum wage job that someone would say was very trivial in and of itself. However, the worker realized that his assignment wasn't by itself. He knew his efforts were linked to a grander plan and that knowledge gave him a sense of pride and increased his desire to perform a higher level. Could it be that many of the followers in the world are doing less than their potential because they can't see how the turning of that screw or the washing of that plate or the filling out of that form impacts the takeoff of aircraft, the feeding of kings and the collection of millions of dollars?

Like everything else in this chapter, a good follower might have to do some legwork to determine the LINKAGE of their ASSIGNMENT and the overall OUTCOME. Again, in my perfect world, every follower would receive this information from their leadership chain. Unfortunately, we're not in my perfect world (as evidenced by the lack of Super Bowl championships for the Dallas Cowboys in the last 20+ years) so if a follower is to be a three-dimensional follower, they are going to have to go the extra mile to determine why their particular ASSIGNMENT is important. And this importance has to be more than just a paycheck because you can find a paycheck anywhere. My emphasis on knowing this LINKAGE is more about motivation than anything else. I'm way passed the notion that people will perform excellently on their jobs just because that's what they are supposed to do. For us Type A personalities, that makes sense. However, we've all worked with some Type B through Z personalities who need more than pride in their job to get anything done, much less to do it well. I believe this motivation lies in the LINKAGE. The knowledge that if I do my job at a high level, something amazing will happen and that if I slack off, disaster may occur, is an incredible motivator. What we do matters and if we don't recognize the ultimate impact of our efforts, we will never know fulfillment in being followers and the grand plans of those employing us will never be realized. We're doing more than cutting stone or earning a paycheck…we are helping someone do something that will impact lives for generations to come.

Taking a 3-D Look at Yourself

1. For your current task, where can you find the GUIDANCE and when was the last time you reviewed that GUIDANCE?

2. For your current task, who defined the OUTCOME?

3. Do you have trouble "staying in your lane?" If I asked those you work with, what would they say about your ability to stay in your lane?

4. Why is your current task important?

Chapter 3: Followers Must Know their ROLE on the Team

Know your role and shut your mouth.
-- Dwayne "The Rock" Johnson

As much as I might hate to admit it, one of my favorite things to watch growing up was wrestling. Then again, I'm not sure why I hate to admit it because I admitted in my first two books that I love comic books… Back to wrestling…I loved it!!! Junkyard Dog…The Road Warriors…Caine…The British Bulldog…Jimmy "Superfly" Snuka…those guys were my soap opera stars. I partied when they won and I wanted to cry when they lost. However, of all of those men, my favorite wrestler was "The Rock." Everyone knows him now as Dwayne Johnson, the star who seems to be in a new movie every month. But to me, he will always be "The Rock." He was strong, fast, from my hometown of Miami and he talked a great game. I would be on the edge of my seat. It wasn't just about watching him wrestle (Although I did love "the people's elbow"). To see him grab the microphone to shout out one of his classic lines like "Can you smell what The Rock is cooking?" (you need to drag that "smell" out for a few sentences to get the full effect) was a thing of beauty. However, the best line came when he would point at another wrestler and say, "Know your ROLE and shut your mouth." With those words, my night was complete and I could go on about my life knowing The Rock had put all things in proper order.

While those words came from an oiled up man in some bikini briefs, they have amazing applicability. Perhaps the biggest issue with followers is that they don't know their ROLE so they just keep talking about anything and everything but their responsibility to the team. The ROLE we are talking about is different than the ASSIGNMENT we mentioned in the previous chapter. The ASSIGNMENT is part of dealing with the task but the ROLE is the obligation the follower has to the team and to the leader. This is an often missed point because we tend to think that as long as the follower is doing their part on the task, their work is done. However, because teams and organizations have multiple personalities involved, a good follower must not only navigate relationship to the task but also must integrate with the team to be successful. The best followers not only do their part to complete the task, they take it on themselves to make the team better.

If a follower pays attention to their RESPONSE, their OBEDIENCE, their LOYALTY and their ENCOURAGEMENT, then they will know their ROLE and they will be at their best in support of the team. Now whether or not they shut their mouths is a situation for another book.

Between stimulus and response there is a space. In that space is our power to choose our response. In our response lies our growth and our freedom.
-- Viktor E. Frankl

Growing up I remember the phrase, "Children should be seen and not heard" being drilled into me. As I went through the various stages of my young life, I would interact with adults who would note by age and assume that I didn't have anything valuable to say. After all, what could an adolescent, a teenager, or a young adult have to add to the conversation? (Right about here someone would say, "This is grown folk's business.") The irony is that as I was getting older, those people got older as well and were never able to look past the relative difference in our ages. Therefore, I was perpetually to remain quiet because I would never be "grown folk." Sadly, what many of us have done to children in our attempts to keep them silent has spilled over in how we treat followers. If they don't have the rank, the office, the education or the title, they should be seen and not heard. The consequence of that mentality is that the followers took the direction to heart and stayed silent. The silence of followers is contrary to the RESPONSE teams and leaders require from team members in order to operate at the highest levels of performance. The organization will never thrive if followers don't give the needed RESPONSE in light of the questions and issues impacting the group.

I will admit this is a tricky issue. We've all experienced cases where the RESPONSE from followers was inappropriate and unhelpful. Therefore, in order to prevent this kind of RESPONSE, many leaders "threw the baby out with the bathwater" and either explicitly or implicitly shut down feedback from their followers. Now, the idea that followers should ever speak up is frowned upon and considered detrimental to the forward motion of the team. However, nothing could be further from the truth. Team members have a responsibility to give a RESPONSE when they see something that could negatively affect the team or could possibly push the team ahead in an unprecedented way. To remain silent is to at best slow the progress of the team, and at worst, cause physical harm to another team member.

At a nationally televised football game, there are cameras everywhere. In an attempt to cover all the action, the network positions cameras in every conceivable place. Some of these cameras are large and prominently positioned while others are seemingly hidden and inconsequential. When there is a significant play like a turnover or determining if someone made a catch, the director doesn't just ask for input from the large sideline cameras. The director essentially asks for every camera to report in to give its unique perspective on the play. For one of the cameras to hold back its view because it doesn't feel like its opinion matters could cause the game to turn without all the pertinent information. In a real sense, every follower is a camera with a unique perspective to the operation of the team. When handled properly, the RESPONSE from these "cameras" will make the team better and enable that team to produce superior results.

This is a point where I have failed as a follower more times than I care to admit. Because of my experience, expertise and particular view of a situation, I've seen things I know the leader is blind to but I've chosen to keep my RESPONSE to myself because "why would she care?" or "it's not my problem." In those cases, the unit had the opportunity to bypass an obstacle or double our output but because I was selfish with my RESPONSE, we suffered adverse consequences and never reached our potential. What I needed to remember then, and remember now, is that it is part of my ROLE to give a RESPONSE but I am not responsible for the leader's or team's reaction to my RESPONSE. Yes, I could give the best idea in the world that the leader ignores. That doesn't mean my RESPONSE was wrong. I played my ROLE and if not following my RESPONSE has undesirable results, the responsibility is not on me but on the leader who made the decision.

Please remember that it's not always what you say but how you say it. A lot of great RESPONSES to the needs of the organization were ignored because of the attitude those RESPONSES came with. If the intent of the RESPONSE is to help the team, then the RESPONSE needs to be packaged in such a way that it can be received and acted upon. Calling the leader stupid for making a certain decision in front of the entire team because you already know the plan will fail is not the way to give a RESPONSE. There are times the RESPONSE needs to be shared in front of the team but there are probably more times when the RESPONSE needs to be taken behind closed doors. With respect to Malcolm X, we have to share our RESPONSE not just by any means necessary but by the means that will have the best effect on the team.

One more thing...another rule I learned in the Air Force was that there are only so many times a follower can look at a leader and say, "but, sir or ma'am." To repeatedly give the same RESPONSE to the same person in the same way is insanity. Therefore, limit yourself to three "but sirs or ma'ams." Give them your RESPONSE in the best way no more than three times and if they still don't want to adjust based off of your RESPONSE, salute smartly and move forward. It is the leader's job to make the decision and if they have settled on the course of action, accept that you have played your ROLE and move on. This is not an excuse to stay quiet though. When another instance to speak up appears, good followers give their RESPONSE. If followers do not share their perspective in their RESPONSE, the team is sure to fail...and then everyone will have something to say, and none of it will be good.

One of the first duties of a Scout is obedience to authority. He must obey his orders in the first place and put his own amusement or desires in the second.
-- Robert Baden-Powell

My dad was in the Air Force when I was born. I followed him around the world for 18 years until I left for college. In college, I spent four years in Air Force ROTC working my way towards a commission. Immediately after graduating college, I entered the Air Force and then spent the next 24 years serving my country. Around year five of my Air Force career I got married and I have been HAPPILY (emphasis added) married for 22 years at the time of writing this book. Why this trip down memory lane you ask? Because living in the house of an Air Force enlisted man, being in college on an Air Force ROTC scholarship, serving in the Air Force as an active duty officer and being married to Linda Payne all have one thing in common...you better learn to be OBEDIENT if you're going to survive. My dad was a perfectionist and his house ran his way and if you wanted to avoid trouble, you better obey. If I wanted to actually have the Air Force pay for my school and give me a commission as a second lieutenant, I had to obey the rules they set forth. In fact, when I got to college they made me take an oath swearing to God that I would, "obey the orders of the officers appointed over me…" While my oath changed when I became in officer, the expectations to obey remained the same. Uncle Sam told me where I could live, what I had to wear and who I could and could not date. To violate those rules was to put my career, and my freedom, in jeopardy. I have to be honest that I don't remember the pastor telling me to obey when I got married but once again, not obeying my wife resulted in severe consequences. All of that to say OBEDIENCE has been a major part of my life and while I certainly haven't mastered followership, I do recognize that if a person is going to be a successful member of any team, they are going to have to practice OBEDIENCE.

Is there any word in the English language that causes more people to shiver than "OBEDIENCE?" Dictionary.com defines the word as "the act or practice of obeying; dutiful or submissive compliance."[3] Oh no they didn't! They used the word "submissive" in the definition. No wonder nobody likes the word. I can hear the shouts from the rafters now, "We are all equal and I don't have to be submissive to anyone!" And I would agree with that. We don't <u>have to</u>.

---

[3] https://www.dictionary.com/browse/obedience, definition 2, accessed 22 October 2018.

However, if we're going to be three-dimensional followers, we should because if a follower isn't OBEDIENT to the organization's rules, the follower will be disruptive to the organization and distract the organization from accomplishing its goal. This is where I draw my analogy between being "grown" and being a "grown-up." You see, grown folks are always talking about what the <u>can</u> do. "I <u>can</u> stay out all night." "I <u>can</u> sleep with that person." "I can wear what I want to wear." On the other hand, "grown-ups" are always talking about what they <u>should</u> do. "I can stay out all night but should I?" "I can sleep with that person but should I?" "I can wear what I want to wear but should I?" We have a lot of followers who are grown but we need followers who are grown-ups because grown-ups recognize the need for "good order and discipline" on the team. These followers, the good ones, prioritize OBEDIENCE to the rules over their own freedoms.

One of the ironies of this OBEDIENCE thing is that most of us demand OBEDIENCE from our fellow followers but want a little wiggle-room for ourselves. We want everyone else to be on time but they need to understand when we are late. We want the rest of the team to follow the company dress code but we want the freedom to express ourselves. By doing this we acknowledge that there are rules and the rules are meant for the good of the team, but we are denying our

ROLE on the team when we refuse to practice OBEDIENCE. And I'm sure we could all talk about when people violated team rules and they destroyed team morale and a perfectly capable and talented team never achieved to the level of its potential. Perhaps every sports fan has a story of a prominent athlete on their favorite team with a ton of talent but a complete disregard for team or league rules. Despite their out-of-this-world skill, their failure to be OBEDIENT hurt the team. These were all-star players, but lousy followers, and we have to be better than that.

When we disagree with the rules, we have to make a decision about whether we will be OBEDIENT for the sake of the team or whether we will just go our own way. Truthfully, there's nothing wrong with making a decision that says I can't follow these rules so I'm going to forego a spot in this organization. If you know you can't, or won't, be OBEDIENT to the rules, do everyone a favor and choose another path. As a leader, there's nothing worse than having to deal with people who are always trying to skirt the rules and attempting to get away with something. I remember near the end of my Air Force career, I would look in the mirror and ask myself if I could "get away with" not shaving that morning. I knew the rule was for me to be clean shaven but I just didn't feel like shaving. I wanted to be able to tell myself that the whiskers on my face were barely noticeable and even if someone did notice, I would most likely outrank them and they would stay quiet. I was trying to justify my disobedience. I had to train myself that if I was asking the question, "Can I get away with it?" that I was already wrong and needed to do what I <u>should</u> and not be satisfied with what I <u>could</u>. OBEDIENCE isn't for the weak. OBEDIENCE is for the strong. Those strong enough to set their own desires aside for the betterment of the team. I have to admit that OBEDIENCE kept me alive in my father's house for 18 years, in the Air Force for 24 years and in my marriage for 22 years and counting. Maybe there's something to this OBEDIENCE thing…

You cannot get me to be disloyal to a friend. You just can't do it. Loyalty is a part of what I live by. I didn't say I was going to be loyal to my friend because he was right. I'm going to be loyal to my friend because he's my friend.
-- Jim Brown

Around May 1, 1997 as I was driving down the road, a woman attempted to make a left turn across a divided highway in front of me and her car died resulting in an accident. I reported the accident and sent my car to the shop to be repaired. About 30 days later, I got my car back and on the way home from a squadron golf tournament, I fell asleep at the wheel and hit another car head on. After being pulled out of the car with the "jaws of life" and sent to the hospital and experiencing a humorous case of "mistaken identity" with my wife, I was treated, released and made it home. As I drifted in and out of consciousness due to some very good pharmaceuticals, I heard my wife make a phone call to our insurance company. Albeit I only heard her half of the conversation but I'm pretty sure it went like this:

> Linda: "Hello. I'd like to report a car accident."
>
> Insurance Company: "Yes ma'am. Will you please give me your account information and I will look you up?"
>
> After Linda passed the account information, the Insurance Company employee says, "Oh ma'am, we already have that accident and it's been taken care of."
>
> To this my wife responds, "No, you don't have THIS accident..." After which my wife goes on to explain my second car accident in a 30-day period.

With that explanation and the reporting of the accident to the folks on base, "Crash" Payne was born. I carried that nickname around with me until I retired from the Air Force. It wasn't the worse nickname you could get so I wore the moniker proudly.

Now while I accepted and eventually grew to love the nickname, my insurance company did not. You see, not only had I had two car accidents in a 30-day period, but these were accidents number six and seven in the 12 years I had been driving. After my wife hung up from the call, I cried because I knew the company was going to drop me and I'd be stuck without car insurance because nobody was going to insure "Crash" Payne. However, the strangest thing happened.

While the company raised my rates to the level of a 16-year old driving a Lamborghini, they never dropped me. I was shocked because they had every reason to cut their losses with me. Heck, I would have cut my losses with me. For reasons I still quite don't understand, the company demonstrated a level of LOYALTY that I had never experienced. Because of their LOYALTY, I have demonstrated an equal amount of LOYALTY and have sworn to never drop the company no matter what other companies promised me.

I took the time to tell that story of LOYALTY because in our uber-transient world, the concept of LOYALTY has gone by the wayside. Everyone is looking for the next big thing, the next best deal and to hell with the team, organization, or company I was just with. This lack of LOYALTY has transformed many groups from being teams with a committed core of workers to a loose conglomeration of part-timers waiting for the "train" to slow down just enough so they can jump off and get on the next one. This continuous churn of followers, and for that fact leaders as well, has left many organizations in a constant state of rebuilding and never achieving their ultimate goals. To reach the utmost in effectiveness, organizations need followers who demonstrate LOYALTY to the organization.

I probably should apologize here because this is the point of the book where I will get the most preachy because LOYALTY is <u>huge</u> to me because LOYALTY is very akin to "faithfulness" which provides the concept of "unswerving allegiance to a leader or organization."[4] I want to know that those who follow me will be there no matter what and I want those who lead me to know that I will be there no matter what. Of course I understand when followers have opportunities for promotion or to obtain different experiences. Growth is supposed to happen. When you've outgrown the pot you are in, you should move to a new pot. My problem is, and continues to be, when people tell you they'll be there and the second trouble arises or they don't get their way, they jump ship and move on like they were never a part of the unit. It's when you're in the foxhole that you need to know who is on your side and way more than I would like, the foxhole gets very empty once the bullet starts flying. It's funny that everyone wants to be a part of the team during the parade but nobody wants to be there during the battle. Those that stay in and through the battle are demonstrating the LOYALTY the team needs to overcome the enemy and claim the victory.

---

[4] https://www.dictionary.com/browse/faithfulness?s=t, synonyms for faithful, accessed on 24 October 2018.

One final "preachy" note. In 2018, the NCAA decided that players who had not played a certain amount of games could transfer from their schools to play football somewhere else without losing their eligibility. This rule was invoked several times during the season as quarterbacks who lost their starting jobs transferred to other teams in order to try to start there. Honestly, I hate it. Now I am not passing judgement on any of those players but I am questioning their LOYALTY to their team. Before the season and while they were starters, they told every interviewer about their love for the university and their plan to win championships for the school. And then all of a sudden, right after the coach announces a new starter at the position, the young man announces that he is leaving for another school so he has a chance to play. What happened to all those flowery words about loving the school? Their words said one thing but their actions said another in regards to LOYALTY. And while I don't doubt that in many ways they are excellent young men with incredible football talent, their demonstrated lack of LOYALTY is concerning to me.

As I climb down off my soapbox, I remind you that all groups are formed with the purpose of reaching the mountaintop. However, we have to remember that there are a lot of challenges on the way to that lofty destination. If followers have no LOYALTY, the team could move forward but it will never reach the heights it is destined for. Good followers don't quit on the team…even when part of the team has been in a number of accidents. Just ask my insurance company…

> *When you encourage others, you in the process are*
> *encouraged because you're making a commitment and*
> *difference in that person's life. Encouragement really does*
> *make a difference.*
> *-- Zig Ziglar*

Growing up I was a huge fan of the Philadelphia 76'ers. Doctor J, Darrell Dawkins, Maurice Cheeks and Andrew Toney were my basketball heroes. I celebrated their every victory and I was devastated by each loss. Of course, as a Sixers fan in those days, as much as I loved the Sixers, I hated the Lakers and the Celtics. These two teams were the bane of my basketball existence because they always seemed to find a way to outplay and outscore my beloved team. While the likes of Bird, Magic, McHale and Kareem garnered all the headlines, there was one guy on the Celtics that drew a huge amount of my ire. His name was Cedric Maxwell. Now, I can't say I ever really saw Cedric Maxwell play in a game but I've heard that in his day, he was an extremely good basketball player. By the time I started watching basketball and he had joined the team in Boston, Father Time had caught up with him and he was a player with a very minor role on a very good team. Why would I be so focused on a guy who spent most of his time on the bench and barely, if ever, showed up in the box score? My frustration with Cedric Maxwell was that he wouldn't just sit on the bench. When the Celtics would start a run or make a big shot, the camera would pan the Celtics sideline and there would be Cedric Maxwell waving that @#$% towel. Even though he wasn't the player he used to be, he was still very engaged in what the team was doing on the court and he had fully accepted the role of ENCOURAGEMENT for the Celtics. It seemed to me that Cedric Maxwell would wave that towel from the opening the tip to the ending buzzer and the more he waved the towel, the more the Celtics won. I wanted someone to run by and grab that towel and flush it down the toilet. However, as I've gotten older I've realized that it wasn't the towel that made the difference. The difference came from the man who decided that his job was to ENCOURAGE his teammates. Larry Bird was the unquestioned leader of the 1980s Celtics but it was followers like Cedric Maxwell who recognized their role of ENCOURAGEMENT that made the Celtics a dynasty.

ENCOURAGEMENT is a direct outcome of the LOYALTY we talked about in the previous section because we stay together in the bad times out of LOYALTY and since we are together, we should choose to "inspire with courage, spirit, or confidence"[5] those around us. Since things will not always go well, there is a requirement for someone inside the organization to reach out and lift the spirit of their teammates. There's nothing more discouraging than watching those we thought were with us leave or turn their backs when we are in the deepest need. But a good follower recognizes that their ROLE expands beyond just getting the job done but in ENCOURAGING their partners to continue the battle to achieve the organization's goals.

An interesting thing about ENCOURAGEMENT comes from the bible. We often hear people quote Hebrews 10:25 by saying, "Forsake not the gathering." These words are usually thrown at people who have decided getting up on Sunday mornings just isn't for them and that they can do this Christian thing without going to church. What we often miss is the "why" we shouldn't forsake the gathering. In context, starting at verse 24, this scripture reads, "And let us consider how we may spur one another on toward love and good deeds, not giving up meeting together, as some are in the habit of doing, but ENCOURAGING one another-and all the more as you see the Day approaching" (Hebrews 10:24-25, NIV, emphasis added). The writer of Hebrews tells us that we don't just get together to sing, be preached at or to give our money. The reason he directs us to come together is

[5] https://www.dictionary.com/browse/encourage, accessed on October 25, 2018.

so that we might ENCOURAGE one another. When you look at who the book of Hebrews was written to, this makes perfect sense. The recipients of this biblical letter were being persecuted and probably felt like giving up on this "Jesus thing." In the midst of this anguish, they receive a letter that says instead of going your own separate ways back to your former lives, keep meeting with one another so you can ENCOURAGE each other to live the lives God has called you to. Interestingly, we can worship alone, pray alone and with technology, we can give alone. However, we can't ENCOURAGE alone. We often need someone else who recognizes what we are going through to remind us of our ability to make it. Yes, the leader should bring ENCOURAGEMENT as well but there is something special about fellow followers making a point to lift the spirits of those around them.

The story is told of a little second grade boy who was trying out for a part in the school play. The day came for the auditions and his mother took him to school and waited for him to come out. She was nervous because he didn't have any real talent. She knew he couldn't sing, act, dance, or memorize things very well. After 45 minutes the boy came out of the audition with a huge smile on his face. "How did it go, honey?" his mom asked. "It was great, Mom," the boy replied. "Guess what? I've been chosen to clap and cheer."

While many of us want to be the lead actor or actress in the organization, we have to realize that all of us, like the little boy in the story, have a ROLE on the team to provide ENCOURAGEMENT to those around us. If we neglect this ROLE, the team will suffer and success is less and less likely. The men and women that we work with need to hear a kind word every once in a while so they will have the courage to stay the course. Perhaps there's nothing better than having a cheering section on the team with us to provide the ENCOURAGEMENT we need during the toughest times. And for my sake, when you ENCOURAGE your team, please do it without a towel so I don't have flashbacks.

Taking a 3-D Look at Yourself

1. What necessary RESPONSE are you withholding saying to your leadership/team? Why are you holding back and what will you do to overcome that obstacle?

2. Do you have trouble being OBEDIENT to leadership or following rules? Why do you think that is? Choose a rule that you have trouble with and commit to obeying that rule for the next 30 days and see if the environment of the team changes.

3. Would the people around you consider LOYALTY to be one of your personality traits? Why or Why not?

4. Who do you work with that could use your encouragement? Be intentional about sharing encouragement with that person several times over the next two weeks.

Chapter 4: Followers Must Know the SOUL of Themselves
Age wrinkles the body. Quitting wrinkles the soul.
-- Douglas MacArthur

In 2006, in the midst of amazing musical performances by the likes of Beyonce Knowles and Jennifer Hudson, perhaps my favorite song in the movie *Dreamgirls* was performed by Eddie Murphy. Eddie played the crooner, James "Thunder" Early, who "the Dreamettes" opened for to launch their career. Because the movie was called "Dreamgirls," it probably goes without saying that as the movie progressed, the Dreamettes become the Dreamgirls and surpass "Thunder" Early in fame and notoriety. Near the end of the movie, and near the end of Jimmy Early's career, he comes out during a show honoring the Dreamgirls and begins to sing a lovely ballad. To the shock of everyone, in the middle of the song, Jimmy stops the band and proclaims that he "can't sing no more sad songs." He then breaks out into a rap with the refrain of "Jimmy got SOUL, Jimmy got SOUL, Jimmy got, Jimmy got, Jimmy got SOUL." The scene is made even funnier as Jimmy strips down to his underwear while singing the song.

OK, I just saw you rolling your eyes wondering why I brought that up. I brought it up because even though the character, James "Thunder" Early was world famous, at the end of his career, he felt like the world didn't understand him and he still didn't know himself. Hence, the repeated line

"Jimmy got SOUL." He wanted everyone to know he was more than the sad songs they had heard from him over the years. Perhaps the reason that song, and that line especially, resonates with me so much is because there have been times in my life that I've wanted to proclaim to people that I was more than what they saw. I had "SOUL" that was untapped and unknown to the watching world. However, before I could share my SOUL with the rest of the world, I had to understand what that SOUL was. Theologically speaking, the SOUL is that part of us that makes us who we are, the seat of our personality and emotions. Until we come to grips with that part of us it's going to be incredibly difficult for anyone else to get to know us and appreciate us for who we are.

I would argue that this responsibility is even greater for followers. When we are in a following role, we tend to expect the leader to just know who we are and draw us out. Unfortunately, the task oriented leaders don't often take the time to get to know us and treat us like a number or a cog in the machine of their organization. To that we feel slighted but we don't give the necessary RESPONSE in that situation which would be to share with them our SOUL. But if we don't know our own SOUL, how will we ever explain who we are to the leadership. In this case, the SOUL the follower needs to know and reveal is their Self-Care, their Objective, their Usefulness and their Limitations. If we do it right, maybe we can explain our SOUL to the world and not have to take our pants off to do it.

> *Honestly, self-care is not fluffy - it's something we should take seriously.*
> *-- Kris Carr*

I was a "latchkey kid" growing up. My mom and dad both worked full time so it was a natural part of life for me to come home from school and handle business around the house until my parents came home. I was responsible for doing homework, taking care of my brother, fixing a snack and completing chores before my parents got home. It's funny that I didn't know anything was wrong with being a latchkey kid until much later in life as people talked about the ills of young people going to empty houses and being forced to handle life on their own. Obviously everybody responds differently to things but being a latchkey kid gave me a sense of responsibility and allowed me to make decisions about time management and task prioritization at an early age. The bottom line is that I learned how to take care of myself. When you add the latchkey nature of my upbringing to my mom's insistence that her son "wouldn't be dependent on any woman," I learned at a fairly young age to do all the things necessary, like cook, wash and clean, to live on my own. Now the irony of the whole situation is that even though I grew up learning how to take care of myself, nobody took much time to teach me about SELF-CARE.

If you're not noticing a difference, bear with me for a moment. For many of us, "taking care of ourselves" simply meant being able to live unsupervised. I didn't need a babysitter because "I could take care of myself." Essentially this meant that I could be left alone and my parents had no fear of the house burning down or me ending up in the hospital. This definition of "taking care of yourself" differs greatly from the concept of SELF-CARE. SELF-CARE consists of the knowledge and application of those things that are required for an individual to remain at their physical, emotional, spiritual and mental peak. While everyone can, and probably should, do the same things to take care of themselves (don't eat the petroleum jelly, drive defensively, don't stick Legos in your nose), SELF-CARE will be different for each individual. I need more sleep than you but you have to listen to jazz to calm down. Somebody just has to run a couple of miles in the morning while another person has to have flowers on their desk. We can't look down on what another person needs for their SELF-CARE simply because it doesn't match our needs.

The reason why knowledge of their own SELF-CARE requirements is important for a follower is that the follower needs to understand the things that are required for them to be their best. This could also help with determining whether or not a follower gets involved with some organizations. Let's say you get a job offer from a trendy organization to do something you love. When you visit the office for the second interview you notice rap music playing. Because you loathe rap music, you are particularly attentive to this and according to your nerves, they play this type of music every day, all day. Because it bothers you so much, you casually mention the music to the interviewer who proudly says they play that music because they feel it inspires creativity in the employees. Here's where SELF-CARE comes in. Rap music makes you grind your teeth so you have to make a decision if you can take a job that requires you listen to rap music during the workday. If you know your SELF-CARE, you also have the opportunity to discuss "work-arounds" to listening to that music. Do they allow you to wear earbuds playing a different type of music? Is there a way to work in an area where you can't hear the music playing? Can they turn the volume down in your area of the work center? Each of these questions is about your SELF-CARE and the answers are very important because they will impact whether or not you will be able to be the best you in that job.

It would be a wonderful world if every organization took into account everything that each individual needs to work at their highest level but those organizations don't exist in the real world. What does exist is the ability of every follower to know what he or she needs to be their best selves and then to do those things to maintain their capacity. When a follower knows their SELF-CARE, the follower can "do the little things" the organization can't or won't do thereby enabling the follower to be their best the predominant amount of time. The challenge for every follower is to be their best no matter what and the process to being their best is rooted in SELF-CARE.

> *When a thing is done, it's done. Don't look back. Look forward to your next objective.*
> *-- George C. Marshall*

I truly enjoyed being the Director of Operations in the 741st Missile Squadron at Minot Air Force Base, ND and the Professor of Aerospace Studies at Air Force ROTC Detachment 605, North Carolina A&T State University in Greensboro, NC. In both these positions I had the opportunity to interact with and mentor some of the finest young men and women the United States had to offer. My job was to supervise and provide guidance to these two disparate groups of people. Even though those in North Dakota were well on their way in their Air Force careers and those in North Carolina were still trying to learn how to put on uniforms, my initial guidance to them was always the same. When they would ask me what I thought they should do next, my answer was always "What is your definition of success?" They were coming to me because I had over twenty years of Air Force experience and I was the leader. However, I knew if they were going to be their best in their current roles as followers, they needed to know where they were intending to go. They needed to know their OBJECTIVE.

The OBJECTIVE for the follower is where they are trying to go in life. I usually told my cadets who were asking me for directions in life that if they tell me where they are trying to go, I can tell them which way to turn. For instance, if you tell me you're going to Disney World, I can make a logical suggestion to get you there. The destination should determine the direction and if a follower doesn't know the destination, they will never know the right direction. This is so important because some people are in positions and have no idea why they are there. I talked about seeing a LINKAGE between a person's individual task and the organization's ultimate goal in Chapter 2. Well, there should be a LINKAGE also between the follower's current job and the OBJECTIVE they have for their lives. This LINKAGE provides a boost to the mental and emotional well-being of a follower and reminds them that the course they are on is right one.

OBJECTIVE was crucial to me in college because without it I never would have graduated. The truth is I didn't want to go to college. I wanted to be an Air Force officer. That was my OBJECTIVE. Well, to be even more truthful, I wanted to be a general in the Air Force. (Major Payne was nice but General Payne? WOO!!!) Unfortunately, to achieve that OBJECTIVE, I had to go to college. College was fine when I was interested in the class. Math, English and History classes were cool because I liked them. Now, Psychology and Sociology on the other hand were miserable and nearly drove me to quit. I wasn't going to quit because they were hard. I was going to quit because I wasn't interested in them. What I had to remind myself of was my OBJECTIVE. To do this I bought a second lieutenant bar and put it on my bulletin board in my dorm room. When I would be studying for a Psychology test and was ready to throw down the book, I would look up at the rank and remember my OBJECTIVE. Psychology wasn't the end but a means to that end and if I didn't pass the Psychology class I would be in danger of losing my scholarship which would be me in danger of leaving school which would eliminate my chance of achieving my OBJECTIVE. All of a sudden Psychology class became much more important. Not because I was interested in anything Freud had to say but because this "current job" was essential to reaching my OBJECTIVE. One of the biggest problems I saw while I was teaching at North Carolina A&T was that most of the students had no OBJECTIVE. Actually, many of them did. Their OBJECTIVE was to "get to college." And since they were enrolled in classes, they had obtained their OBJECTIVE and nothing more needed to be done. That explains all those 1.2 GPAs I saw. They didn't know where they were going so they were very unimpressive in their current jobs as students. A lot of followers fall into this trap and because they aren't trying to go anywhere, they don't perform very well where they are.

Please know this isn't about jumping to the next best thing at the earliest opportunity. This is being judicious about the tasks you take on because they provide the chance you need to get to your ultimate destination. A biblical proverb spoken by Jesus says, "Whoever is faithful in very little will be given much" (Luke 16:10). The vast majority of people I've talked to about their definition of success or their OBJECTIVE has talked about how they wanted much. Heck, Bobby Payne wanted to be a general…that's much. However, to obtain that much, that OBJECTIVE, we have to be willing to do the little which means being the best we are at the position we are at so we can receive and achieve the much we desire. A follower without an OBJECTIVE is just like a car with the engine revving but the parking brake on…they are going nowhere fast. They are making a lot of noise but all they are producing is sound and smoke (ooh, that was good. Sounds like a few people I've known throughout the years.) To be

the best where they are at, a follower needs to know where
they are going…they need to know their OBJECTIVE.

*Joy, feeling one's own value, being appreciated and loved by
others, feeling useful and capable of production are all factors
of enormous value for the human soul.
-- Maria Montessori*

In 2005 my family and I moved to Colorado Springs, CO
where I took a job working for an Air Force organization
charged with acquiring new weapon systems for the service.
There was a lot of exciting activity going on but unfortunately
I was assigned to a rather boring part of the office to a couple
of programs that were pretty much moving on autopilot. As
I sat in my cubicle hoping for something to happen with my
programs, I would overhear others in the office talking about
the analysis they were doing on this futuristic system and how
they were going to have to do all these studies to determine
the optimal solution. Those words were poetry to me
because 10 years earlier I completed my degree in Operations
Analysis. Sadly, that wasn't the project I was assigned so I sat
in my corner with my Master's degree trying to hit the end of
the Internet. About a year into the job I got another
assignment and was preparing to leave that organization. I
made an appointment to talk to the Colonel in charge to get a
little career guidance. The first thing he did was sit me down
facing a white board and he asked what I had done and what
my experience was. I rattled off a couple of assignments and

he wrote them down on the board. Then I mentioned that I went to the Air Force Institute of Technology and earned a Master's degree in Operations Analysis. He had started writing as I talked but then when he got about to the word "operations" he stopped and looked at me. With a stunned look on his face, he said to me, "I've had you in the wrong section this whole time." At that moment, this Colonel recognized my USEFULNESS. Unfortunately, because I was such a lousy follower at the time, I kept my USEFULNESS to myself for that entire year and never helped the organization achieve its desired end.

Actually, according to this book, I failed in that situation at least twice. I failed to give the necessary RESPONSE when I heard my teammates struggling over a problem I had solved in graduate school and I failed to let them know that I had skills and abilities that could help in the accomplishment of that task. To this day I don't know why I remained silent. I knew the material and I believe I was good at it. But for whatever reason, since my supervisor didn't read my mind and put me in the right position, I decided they didn't need to benefit from my USEFULNESS. No doubt that I was the exact opposite of a good follower in that job.

Since we should know ourselves better than anyone else, we should know our USEFULNESS. What do we do better than anyone else? What knowledge, skills and abilities do we bring to the fight that can enhance the capabilities of the organization? If you've ever been on a job interview, you've heard those questions. Regrettably, many of us downplay our USEFULNESS due to some false sense of humility and we, nor our team, ever reach their full potential. For whatever reason our focus seems to dwell on our weaknesses rather than those things that make us USEFUL. And because we are focused on what we can't do, we never get around to doing what we can do. Again, that is detrimental to the follower and the team.

When a follower understands their USEFULNESS they can maximize their effectiveness on tasks and assignments. This is not to say that we should shirk away from things that don't come easy to us but it is to say that we also shouldn't cower from opportunities to walk in our gifts and be our best. When an assignment comes up that fits our USEFULNESS as followers, we should volunteer without hesitation. It still boggles my mind that people who are good at something won't raise their hand to do it when the chance presents itself. Perhaps it's all those years in school of being told we are making everyone else look bad because we are answering all the questions. Those memories have obviously stuck with us and now that we are older and the boss mentions an assignment that everything in us wants to do, we look around sheepishly not wanting to stand out. That, my friends, is lousy followership. Three-Dimensional followers have to know their USEFULNESS and strive for opportunities to be USEFUL on behalf of the team at every opportunity. We can't be good followers if we're never doing what we are good at.

> *The man with insight enough to admit his limitations comes*
> *nearest to perfection.*
> *-- Johann Wolfgang von Goethe*

When I went to my first interview with Hardee's back in 1985, the man across the table asked me "What are your weaknesses?" At sixteen, in many ways, I was the walking definition of "weaknesses" but there was no way he was going to get me to admit that to him. Heck, at the time, I wasn't willing to admit any of my weaknesses to myself. As far as anyone knew, I was the smartest, fastest, and strongest 16-year old in Niceville, FL. That was my story and I was sticking to it. On later interviews, when the question changed from "What are your weaknesses?" to "What are your LIMITATIONS?" my answer stayed the same. Weaknesses and LIMITATIONS were bad and there was no way I was telling anyone bad things about me. However, as 49-year old me looks back, I can see how my unwillingness to admit my LIMITATIONS prevented me from being as effective a follower as I could have been because not only does a three-dimensional follower need to understand their

USEFULNESS, they need to understand their LIMITATIONS. To discount either is to set themselves up for failure.

Now, I will readily admit a person looking for a job shouldn't walk into the interview screaming at the top of their lungs that they have trouble getting to places on time and can't add their way out of a paper bag. However, that person needs to understand their LIMITATIONS to the point of determining if the position they are being asked to fill is a good fit for them and whether or not they can compensate for those LIMITATIONS. Through the years I've seen too many people join teams and take jobs that weren't right for them because those positions required a large amount of work be done in the area of their greatest LIMITATION. It's incredibly difficult to be your best as a follower if the assignment you have requires you stare at your LIMITATIONS every day. The level of frustration would certainly inhibit any production. And if you're anything like me (man, I hope not), when you see something on the job that speaks to a LIMITATION, you avoid that task like the plague. Unfortunately, a follower who only does half their job leaves a lot to be desired and will eventually be replaced. This seems like good place for a personal confession. I absolutely love being a pastor. The opportunity to invest myself in the lives of others and preach and teach the word of

God gives me a high like nothing I have ever done. There is an excitement to every moment I get to fulfill that role. At least there's excitement until I have to do the administrative side of the job. As much as I love the preaching, teaching and encouraging parts of my job, I detest the paperwork part. While I have been unable to prove this biblically, I have a strong sense that meetings and paperwork were the works of Satan that got him kicked out of heaven. Therefore, I have a severe LIMITATION when it comes to paperwork. This is where simultaneously being a leader and follower collide. As the leader of St Mary AME, I can ignore this LIMITATION and focus solely on what I love to do. However, as a follower of the Bishop of the 8th Episcopal District of the AME Church, I know that if I want to stay the pastor of St Mary AME Church, I'm going to have to overcome this LIMITATION. The Bishop certainly approves of my preaching, teaching and encouraging but if I'm not submitting my reports on time, he's going to find someone else who can get the entire job done, and not just the part they are good at. Therefore, even though I still don't think I'm the best administrator, I work at it because I want to be the best leader AND follower I can be.

A follower must understand their LIMITATIONS and determine the best way to compensate for those LIMITATIONS. Perhaps this is the worst part for many of us because it means we have to ask for help. The great thing about being on a team is that our LIMITATIONS are most likely strengths of someone else. This means if we will reach out to those we work with, we can develop a sense of interdependence where every task gets done well and the team ultimately succeeds. As a fan of the Los Angeles Dodgers, I watched the 2018 World Series with great disgust. However, as a person fascinated by leadership and followership, I was very intrigued by how Red Sox manager Alex Cora used his outfielders. The 2018 Red Sox had four very good hitting outfielders but one of them, JD Martinez, was considered a defensive liability. This issue wasn't a problem during the regular season for the most part because Martinez could play as the designated hitter and avoid his LIMITATION in the outfield. Where the issue presented itself was during the World Series in games played in Los Angeles. What would Alex Cora do? Playing Martinez regularly in the outfield could be detrimental to the team's defensive efforts but to leave his bat on the bench could be equally damaging to the team's offense. What Cora did, and what Martinez agreed to be a part of, was ingenious. When Martinez started in the outfield, the team would move him from left field to right field and vice versa depending on the hitter. These moves would lower the chances that Martinez would see action in the outfield. The reason this plan excited me so much is because Martinez had to let the world see his

LIMITATION. Yes, this LIMITATION was the topic of multiple news stories, but to be moved around during the game to essentially avoid the ball coming to you had to be very humbling. One thing I never saw, or heard about, was Martinez complaining about being moved around almost on every batter or letting this LIMITATION distract him from what he does best. Oh how I wish he did get distracted because then he wouldn't have been hitting home runs against my team. In this case, what appeared to be a loss for me and the Dodgers was a tremendous example of followership for us all. When a follower knows their LIMITATIONS but doesn't get caught up in them, they can be exceptional and even win a World Series title.

Taking a 3-D Look at Yourself

1. List the things you need to do for SELF-CARE to ensure you are your best physically, mentally, emotionally and spiritually. Are you doing these things? If not, why not?

2. What is your definition of success in the position you are in right now? What is your definition of success in life?

3. What is your USEFULNESS to your current organization? What can you do to help the organization be better and do better? Have you shared your strengths with your leadership?

4. What are your LIMITATIONS? What are you doing to compensate for them?

Chapter 5: So Now What?

A leader I greatly respect gave me this story years ago:

Two cousins grew up side by side from the day they both entered the world. They learned to crawl and toddle together, and later how to run and swim and play ball and all the other things boys do together. They were constant and devoted friends.

But eventually they began to drift apart, as sometimes happens as even good friends move through life. One cousin took to his books, found a certain delight in learning, studied hard, and passed his exams with flying colors. The other cousin decided books weren't such good companions. He skipped school a good bit so he could continue to swim and play ball, ignored his lessons, and ended up failing his exams.

As is usually the way of the world, fortune rewarded the first cousin, who ended up becoming an adviser to the king himself. The second cousin soon found himself employed as an oarsman on his majesty's royal yacht.

One day the king and all his royal advisers embarked on a journey up the river. They sat under a wide canopy in the bow of the boat, where the breeze was best, and discussed affairs of state as the yacht moved along.

The sight of his cousin sitting at ease with royalty irked the oarsman no end. "Look at that lazy fellow, lounging there in the shade, while I must break my back in the sun," he thought as he rowed. "What gives him the right to sit up there, any more than me? After all, aren't we both God's creatures?"

The more he thought about it, the angrier he grew. "Look at those useless louts," he began grumbling to his fellow oarsmen. "They call themselves

advisers, but all they do is sit and gab. Why
should we sweat so hard to push their carcasses
against the current? There's nothing fair about it.
They ought to be back here rowing too. Aren't we
all God's creatures?"
That evening, they tied to shore to make camp.
Everyone ate and fell asleep quickly. The oarsman
woke in the middle of the night to find a firm hand
shaking him by the shoulder. It was the king
himself.
"There's a strange noise coming from over there,"
he said pointing. "I can't get to sleep from
wondering what it is. Please go find out."
The oarsman jumped off the boat and ran up a
hill. He came back a few minutes later.
"It's nothing, Your Majesty," he said. "A cat has
just given birth to a litter of noisy kittens."
"Ah, I see," said the king. "What kind of
kittens?" The oarsman had not looked to see.
He ran up the hill again and came back.
"Siamese," he said. "And how many kittens are
there?" the king inquired. Again, the oarsman
had not noticed. He went back. "Six kittens,"
he reported. "How many males and how many
females?" the king asked. The oarsman ran back
once again. "Three males and three females," he
cried, beginning to lose his breath. "I see," said the
king. "Come with me." They tiptoed to the bow of
the boat, where the king woke the oarsman's
cousin.
"There's a strange noise up on that hill," he told
him. "Go find out what it is." The adviser
disappeared into the darkness and returned in a
moment. "It is a newborn litter of kittens, Your
Majesty," he said. "What kind of kitten?" the
king asked. "Siamese," answered his adviser.
"How many?" "Six." "How many males and
how many females?" "Three males and three
females. The mother gave birth in an overturned

barrel just after we arrived. The cats belong to the
mayor of the village. He hopes they have not
disturbed you, and invites you to come take your
pick if the court is in need of a royal pet."
The king looked at the oarsman. "I overheard
your grumbling earlier today," he said. "Yes, we
are all God's creatures. But all God's creatures
have work to do. I had to send you to shore four
times for answers. My adviser went only once.
That is why he is my adviser, and you must row
the boat.

I have always loved this story. In fact, I loved it so much that I gave it to everyone who worked for me and the cadets I commissioned into the Air Force. A copy of this story also hangs next to the computer in my office at work. This story it is about followership and it challenges me every time I read it. The challenge comes from the fact that while I want to see myself as the advisor, I know more often than not that I have been the oarsman. I've been in a position on the "lower level" of the totem pole and instead of understanding the LINKAGE of what I was doing and exceling in my current ASSIGNMENT, I decided to not demonstrate LOYALTY and not offer ENCOURAGEMENT but chose to whine and moan about how bad things were. Like the oarsman, I never clarified my OBJECTIVE to build on my USEFULNESS but instead gave the negative RESPONSE that everyone should be doing the "harder" work. And then when an opportunity to step up presented itself, I tried to show OBEDIENCE but

68

never understood the GUIDANCE and OUTCOME of the task, and ultimately illustrated my LIMITATIONS. The bottom line is I was a poor follower because in each dimension, I failed. I failed to know the GOAL of my task or recognize my ROLE on the team or understand my own SOUL and not only did I suffer, my team suffered.

At this point I call to mind the phrase from our friends at Alcoholics Anonymous. They will be the first to tell us that "the first step to recovery is admitting you have a problem." If the first step to recovery is admitting you have a problem, then the second step has to be doing something about what we've admitted. Too often we're good at admitting our failures and then just stopping there. It's time we move beyond just confession to transformation. Transformation begins with deciding on the type of follower we want to be and taking the steps that will move us in that direction. In this process we have to keep in mind that it is direction, not decision, that determines destination. In one of the Brady Bunch episodes, the kids sang a song with the line that says, "When it's time to change, you've got to rearrange, who you are and what you're going to be."

Well, because I want to find success while others are driving, I am willing to stand and say, "My name is Bob Payne and I have a problem with followership. I want my own way and I want to do my own thing. I have ignored the GOAL, my ROLE and my SOUL and today I start making the changes necessary to be my best where I am, to be a good follower, to be a three-dimensional follower." I'm going to sit down now because I think it's your turn. Do you have something to say or do you just want to stagnate in the backseat and never know the success meant for you to have? Now that I think about it, I guess when it comes to your followership, you're actually in the driver's seat. Which way will you turn?